Fire Skills

50 Methods for Starting Fires without Matches

By David Aman

Photographs by Victoria Aman

All rights to this book, any information included

And any photographs are copyrighted

Dedication

I would like to dedicate this book to

My beautiful wife

Susan Mertz Aman

Introduction

There are many books about camping and survival that give you general knowledge that you would need to know about when you find yourself up a creek without a paddle. This book focuses in on methods of starting a fire without matches. I have included 50 methods that anyone can do. I have included primitive along with unusual modern methods just to give you a taste of what is possible. If you gain the knowledge then you will have the ability to make a fire in your own personal worst case scenario.

This book was written to give everyone ideas and knowledge to start fires without matches. There are literally hundreds of ways of starting fires without the match. People have been doing it since we all lived in caves. In modern times we have many more resources available to us than primitive man had. We just have to look around and think a little sideways sometimes. There are resources all around you to start fires without matches. Here are fifty methods that, once learned, can help you "be prepared' as we like to say in the Boy Scouts.

This is an excerpt from my book about fire that I hope to have published. If you want to learn more then you should check out my complete work. I have been a Boy Scout leader for 15 years now and starting fire without matches has grown into an obsession for me. I cannot sing worth a darn but I can teach you how to start a fire using dozens of methods. Enjoy but do these things at your own risk!

General advice;

1. Use tinder that is very dry. When you find some or prepare some, store it away for when you need to start a fire. You will be happy that you did

2. A cigarette makes great tinder. Even the paper is meant to light easily. Take the smoldering cigarette and place it in to your birds nest.

3. Blow onto smoldering tinder or the first fragile flames very gently. You do not want to blow the little amount of heat that is there away from the tinder that is not lit yet.

4. Practice these methods when you don't need them. Not only will you learn little tricks and gain experience but you will learn that these methods are not easy or always possible and hopefully this will prompt you into always being prepared with a supply of dry matches.

5. A birds nest is a wad of tinder material that is as thin as a hair and made into a fluffy ball

6. For starting fires with any of the solar methods you want a nice bright sun as close to noon as possible so that the sun is not at a steep angle. It is difficult to use these methods on a partly cloudy day.

7. Keep your tinder warm and dry. You are trying to bring it up to ignition temperature and having it warm already helps a lot.

Safety rules for campfires;

1. Always know how you are going to put your fire out and have something nearby to do it with.

2. Build a fire no larger than necessary

3. Clear fire area of any combustibles down to solid fireproof surface

4. Be careful of high winds

5. Look up for anything that may catch fire

6. Do not leave fires unattended

7. Be absolutely sure that the fire is completely out before leaving camp

8. Don't build fires when you are alone

9. Don't "play" with fire

10. Use fireplaces to enclose a fire if necessary.

11. Break matches in two before throwing them away

Rules for fire building;

1. Put your fireplace in a spot where fire will not spread.

2. Have all of the wood that you will need within easy reach before lighting your match

3. Place your tinder on the side that will catch the wind

4. Have some kindling loosely laid over your tinder pile with an opening left to put the match through to light the tinder

5. Feed the fire. Do this gently, placing the pieces of kindling where the flames are. Put plenty of kindling on but don't smother your flames. Don't get burnt but put the sticks in the right area. You cannot just throw the sticks on. They should be placed on the fire in the spot that will get the flame but leaving air space. A criss-cross design.

1. Flint composite

Getting a good spark or bad spark often comes down to the things you are using to get the sparks from. It can also be from the humidity in the air. There are Flint composites on the market that create good sparks for starting fire with. What you usually find for sale is a carbonium spark stick. They often come with a short piece of steel to scrape against them. The steel scrapes off some of the flint composite and the friction causes the tiny pieces to ignite into sparks. This is the opposite of what happens when steel is struck against real flint. Here, the steel is actually coming off as a glowing shard. By the way, these sparks are excellent signaling devices in the dark and can even be done while wearing mittens.

The magnesium block that they sell in stores has a piece of flint composite on the side. You make a pile of magnesium shavings and then hit the pile with a spark. The magnesium burns at 5,000 degrees F (92,700 degrees C.). Some of these blocks are really made out of a mixture of aluminum and magnesium. These blocks are fireproof when they are in chunk form. They have to be scraped into a powder.

Flint composites are often a composition of iron and cerium and produce very hot sparks. This is what is in a cigarette lighter.

Catch the sparks on fine steel wool "000" or "0000". The wick of a jewelers' alcohol lamp is also one of the best spark catchers. On a brand new wick, light one end and then put it out so that it is charred already and dip the other end of the wick in glue to stop it from fraying.

Starting a fire with a flint composite is very easy. I have taught hundreds of 10 year olds how to do it and they master it in about 10 minutes. I think it is very important for them to succeed right away or else they get discouraged and just walk away, never to try again. If they succeed then they will be confident enough to try again but when the conditions are not so easy. To make their first try successful I have them practice making sparks first of all and then have them make the sparks into a pile of fluffed up oakum. Oakum is a plumbing product that is used to seal joints around cast iron vent pipes. Some oakum comes with a type of oil on it that catches fire very easily.

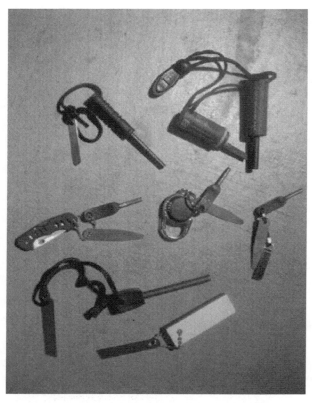

Place the fluffed up pile of oakum on the ground where the wind won't blow it away and place your right hand that is holding the steel (if you are right handed) onto the pile of tinder keeping the steel raised in the air an inch or so above the tinder. Your right hand that is holding the steel should be resting on top of the tinder and resting on the ground. By placing your hand on the ground you can more easily control this hand. YOU DO NOT MOVE THE HAND THAT IS HOLDING THE STEEL! You hold the flint composite in your left hand

and press it tightly against the bottom of the steel. To make sparks you draw your hand that is holding the flint composite backwards. The reason you do not move the hand that is holding the steel is to direct the sparks into the tinder. You do not want your sparks going everywhere. When you draw your flint composite backwards you end up showering all of the sparks right onto the tinder. If you are using oakum the tinder pile will burst into flames with a lot of "ooooh's" and "aaaah's" from the people that are watching.

The mistakes that people make are first of all they work the flint composite and the steel as if they are whittling. They hold the flint steady while drawing the steel against and away from it. They are moving the hand that is holding the steel. They may get plenty of sparks but have a hard time directing them into their tinder. Another mistake is that they cannot get sparks. They should press the flint and steel harder together and try adjusting the edge of the steel so that the sharpest edge is against the flint. A small pocket knife, a knife that has little grooves on the blade or the back of the blade work well to get plenty of sparks. Brand new flint composites have a coating on them that will take a few scrapings to get it off.

The sparks from these fire steels are 3000°C (5500°F) and they work wet or dry. You can get 3000 strikes from one stick.

The flint striker that the Boy Scouts use these days is actually a magnesium/flint alloy that produces a lot of superheated sparks.

When the spark is lying in the birds nest gently blow on it when the nest is raised above your mouth. Blowing down on it will get smoke in your eyes.

Make the birds nest into a bowl into which you put your tinder and glowing spark. The amount of smoke produced and the sound that your birds nest makes just before it bursts into flames is very unique.

2. Flint and steel

Percussive fire starting, i.e. using flint and steel appeared around 5,000 years ago in Europe. For eons, man has carried his flint and steel around to start his cooking fires with. Everyone from Roman soldiers to explorers would protect these important tools from being lost.

One benefit of using hardened steel and a sharp flint stone is that they don't have any moving part to break.

The steel used can be anything from the back of your sheath knife, a hunk of iron or iron pyrite (fool's gold). As a general rule though, steel is a luxury item that is rarely found in nature. Plain old high-carbon steel like an old file make great steels for making sparks.

Flint is an even grained stone that is very hard and sharp. You don't have to use flint though. You can use other hard stones like quartz, jasper, agate, iron pyrites, chert, or jade. Actually any silica stone will do. Break them into chunks that have sharp edges.

The sparks that are created are very short lived and getting them to land on char cloth or other tinder takes a little talent. With a loose-jointed-wrist action, strike the sharp edge of the stone with the steel hard, trying to get sparks to fly off. Try hitting at slightly different angles to find the right approach that makes the best sparks. The sparks are actually small pieces of hot steel flaking off. This metal is superheated to combustion by the concussive force of the blow against the flint.

Hold the flint, quartz or chert in your left hand with a piece of char cloth on top of it near the upwards pointing sharp edge of the rock. Keep the charcloth 1/32" back from the edge of the flint. Hold your steel at a 45 degree angle and hit the flint by swing at a 35 degree angle. You bang down on the edge of the flint with your steel in a downwards motion trying to cause a spark to land onto your char cloth. You can actually make your char cloth go up and over this edge of the flint and beat your steel in the same motion which will cause the cloth to split open at this upper sharp edge of the flint. The advantage of this is that the char cloth is right there to catch the spark. Don't worry about the edge of the flint being covered and not allowing the steel to spark against the flint. It will cut right through the cloth in the first strike or two.

Some experts hold the tinder, especially if it is windy and the tinder is a powder, in the cup of their hand that they are holding the flint with. This way the sparks land in a wind protected area and the tinder doesn't blow around.

You can hold the tinder under your shoe and hold the flint up against your shoe. Bang the steel in a downward motion, propelling the spark into the tinder. (Sounds real simple doesn't it?)

3. Bic lighter that has no fuel

When you can't "flick your Bic" any longer because it has run out of fuel, don't throw it away. You can cram some tinder into the top of it and have the sparker start your tinder on fire. This only works if your tinder is extremely flammable like a gas soaked rag. If you are trying to light shredded cedar bark though you will have to do things a little differently. Don't let the tinder clog up the area between the wheel and the flint.

Carefully take the metal housing that surrounds the area where the flame normally would be. Be careful not to accidentally disturb the metal wheel or the spring loaded flint that is just below it. Fluff up your tinder and place one edge of your tinder pile near but not touching the base of the wheel. Watch the sparks as you spin the wheel and adjust your tinder accordingly.

Another way to light your tinder with "spent" butane lighters is to fluff up your tinder and place it on a hard surface. Elongate your pile of tinder into more than just a pile. Gently run the wheel of the lighter across this tinder while pushing the wheel against the hard surface. Hopefully, this will create sparks as you move the lighter across the hard surface. Take your lit tinder and put it into your prepared firelay. Two things to remember; your lighter is now very fragile and this method will not work forever so try to not let your fire go out.

4. Propane torch lighter

The sparker used for lighting propane torches for soldering makes a great fire lighter. It is light and will give you a hundred chances to light your tinder. It can be used with one hand and the tinder can be placed right inside of the bowl with the flint.

The replacement flints for these torch sparkers' works well by itself. Maybe not conveniently well but it is so small that it will not get in the way. Take a small eye hook and file the tip of it away. Take a pair of pliers and twist the eye hook into the screw in end of the flint replacement. Once together, you have a possible way of starting fires with you always. You could also drill a 1/16 hole through he metal end, put a small split ring through the hole and then attach this fire lighter to your pocket knife or jacket zipper. Attach it to your pocket knife and you won't even know it's there.

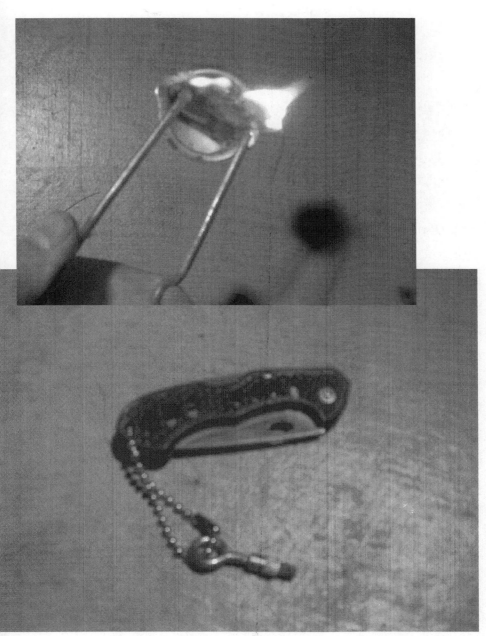

5. Static

While speaking of ways of starting fires with a spark, it once occurred to me as I got up from the couch and got shocked when opening the fireplace doors with a static spark whether it was possible to start a fire this way. I taped a piece of char cloth against the metal of the fireplace and would point my finger at it whenever I left the couch. The static spark just went through the char cloth without any effect. The solution turned out to be isopropyl alcohol. Two drops of this onto the char cloth and the next static spark was all it took to get a flame. This is not catching a spark like I had hoped for but it did start a fire with electricity built up while being lazy watching one of those survival shows. I am sure that gasoline would work just as well but it would make the room smell unpleasant and the wife might yell at you like she does to me. "You're not starting fires in the house again are you? If you burn our house down, I will kill you."

I don't know if you have read the warnings but you will see that they warn you against using cell phones while pumping gas. Somehow they create a spark.

They also say that the static charge that you built up while driving could cause the gas fumes to ignite. Hold the nozzle against the vehicle or gas can as you are pumping to allow any built up static to just flow out of you rather than create a spark.

6. Blast match

A blast match is a flint and steel fire starter that is designed to create many sparks with one hand. It has a retractable large piece of flint composite and a hunk of steel that your thumb pushes on. Gently place the tip of the flint against something hard, push hard against the steel so that it is pressing onto the flint and then use your hand to push the entire unit forward against the rock. This will create a giant shower of sparks. When you lift up and release the pressure against the steel, a spring pushes the flint back out. Don't be tempted to jam the flint quickly against the rock, in and out many times quickly. This will damage the flint. If you are teaching kids how to use this then you should watch them because they will be tempted to make this mistake. Once you have seen one of these in action you will feel that "you just gotta have one of those".

7. Car battery

Sparks can also be accomplished by using jumper cables and your car battery. You could use a piece of wire, like a section of a barbed wire fence to do the same thing. You can also take two wrenches or screwdrivers and cause sparks at your car battery by touching one wrench to the positive terminal and the other to the negative terminal and then touching the tools together for a quick moment. Don't create sparks near the battery if you can help it because the sparks can create an explosion from leaking hydrogen. Don't leave them touching or else you will short out the battery. Cover up your car's engine with a coat or car mats if you have to make the sparks under the hood.

Fluffed up tinder like your cotton t-shirt that you shredded while shivering in the car should work. A gasoline covered rag will definitely work in catching fire from these sparks. The most dangerous part of starting a fire this way is when you actually get a flame. Get it away from your engine that has all of those flammable liquids.

8. Spark plug

If you have a socket wrench, you can remove one spark plug and lean it against the engine block of your car while it is connected to the spark plug wire and you will get a good spark when the key is turned. The base of the spark plug has to be touching the metal part of the engine somewhere. This will obviously start a gas soaked rag on fire. The dangers are many in doing this though. You will be dealing with a rag that is a blaze with gasoline on fire (don't set yourself on fire please) and the fan and fan belt will be turning when you turn the key (don't cut off your hand please).

If you are alone doing this you are in real danger. If the rag does catch on fire you will have to run around the car door and quickly reach under the hood, grabbing something that has serious flames and take it to wherever you have your firelay.

Starting a fire with a spark plug is much easier from a lawn mower. After taking out the spark plug, lay the bottom end over tinder but up against the metal part of your lawn mower. When you pull on the starting cord you will be sending sparks onto your tinder. If you aren't getting any sparks then adjust your spark plug and make sure that the bottom "J" shaped piece of metal of the spark plug is touching the metal on the mower. Remember that the spark plug wire has to still be connected to the spark plug. Also, make sure that you did not accidentally smash the "J" shaped piece of metal so that it is touching the little tip under the spark plug. There is supposed to be a gap between the two. Don't adjust this gap unless they are touching and then spread them apart so there is an ever so slight gap between them.

9. Magnifying lens

We all did it as kids. Burn ants on the sidewalk or get a leaf to smolder using a magnifying glass. When you start fires using one of the solar methods, you are focusing sunlight into a very fine point. This can be done by concentrating the sunlight into a point by having it pass through something or by reflecting backwards into a point. You are trying to intensify the sun's rays onto a single point on your tinder. A magnifying glass will focus sunlight into a point; it shines a dot on the tinder. Maybe you brought a magnifying glass with you to study fossils, plants or insects. A magnifying glass can be found or made. Store bought magnifying glasses are cheap and can usually be found in the school supply section of the store. A magnifying lens is sometimes called a burning glass.

Most magnifying glasses are convex lenses. A 2" lens will start a fire on most sunny days. Smaller lenses may need a bright, sunny, hot day though. You should not have a problem concentrating the sun to a single point long enough to heat up our tinder. You can steady your hand against the ground or a rock to maintain the correct position of the magnifying lens. You could actually rig up some sort of holder for your magnifying glass to hold it in the proper position. The sun only moves about 1 degree every four minutes and that is usually long enough to bring your tinder up to ignition temperature. The object is to focus the sunlight into a single point. It concentrates the heat of the sun enough to start your tinder afire. Move the tinder or the magnifying glass in and out and try tipping it left and right in order to find the perfect point of sunlight. Give the tinder some time to really catch on fire after it starts smoking. Use the glowing tinder to start your "birds nest" on fire

You really don't want to have to count on starting

your fire with a magnifying glass if you can help it. There may be no sun. You always seem to need a fire the most when it is dark, raining or snowing out. If you do get your fire started with a magnifying glass, I wouldn't let it go out. Keep the fire going and carry the fire with you if you have to travel. A magnifying lens is just another piece of glass on a cloudy day or at night.

10. Make up mirror

I bought my make up mirror down at the dollar store. It's about 4" in diameter and has a magnifying power of times 5. It is supposed to be used to put mascara on or to get something out of your eye but I use it to start fires. While on vacation in North Carolina, I found that the bright sunshine on a warm April afternoon allowed me to start a fire in 2 seconds with a wad of cotton held at the focal point from the mirror.

Make the tinder come to somewhat of a point and make the wad of tinder long and narrow. You want the area close to the point of your tinder to be over the obvious focal point without blocking the sun. Simply aim the mirror towards the sun and adjust the tinder's distance from the mirror going towards the mirror and away from the mirror until you have a pinpoint of sunlight touching the tinder. Continue holding it there until you get quite a bit of smoke. This means that many of the fibers of your tinder are smoldering, the more fibers that are smoldering, the better chance you have of blowing them into a flame.

Obviously, the more heat you have generated, the easier it is to get a flame.

11. Headlight

The headlight on your car is a great reflective surface to direct sunlight onto your tinder. The biggest problem you will have is getting the stupid thing out of its resting place without breaking it. Sure, it's not really that hard when you have the proper wrenches and screwdriver. If you are lacking the tools then try shoving a stick, or better yet, the tire iron that comes with your car to take the hub caps off into the gap between the car and the headlight housing. There are usually four screws that hold the headlight in place and these will have to be broken. Once you have the headlight out of off of the car then remove the light bulb by twisting it and pulling it out from the back. Slide your tinder through this hole and point the entire face of the headlight towards the sun. You may find this easier than other reflective methods because of how big the headlight is. Make sure to have your fire lay ready to accept a flame before even starting. Adjust the tinder in and out while focusing the headlight onto the sun's rays. What you are trying to end up with is a focused point of sunlight on your tinder. Wait a few seconds after it the tinder starts to smolder and smoke before carefully pulling it out of the back, raising the tinder above your head slightly and gently blow the smoldering tinder into flames.

12. Flashlight

Using, a flashlight reflector that is 2" in diameter to start a fire is a real challenge. I used very fine tinder and stuck it through the back of the hole where the light bulb went. I then pointed the reflector towards the sun. On the inside of the reflector you could see circles that were reflections of the sun being reflected off of the other side of the reflector. Theses circles would be oblong, being bigger on one side of the center hole than the other. When I moved the flashlight reflector this way and that, I could get the reflected circle centered perfectly with the light bulb hole. Now I knew that I was pointing the reflector directly at the sun.

I pulled the tinder in and out of the hole slightly, watching the bright point of light until it was at the tip of the tinder. This would cause the tinder to smolder immediately but would not light it on fire. I found that I had to twist the tinder into a tight point and feed it through the hole a little at a time allowing more and more of it to catch the suns heat and smolder. Eventually I had burnt the fine tip of my tinder away and the diameter of the part that was smoldering was the size of the diameter of the light bulb hole. Having my birds nest ready, I placed the smoldering tinder into it, folded the birds nest gently around it and blew it into flames.

I have found that the best tinder to use the reflector of a flashlight to start fires with is an average cigarette. You can stick a cotton swab through the hole and have the reflected sunlight start the cotton swab on fire.

13.Ice

You can also make a magnifying glass from ice. Cut a piece of clear ice into a circle and shave it with your knife into the approximate shape of a magnifying glass. Use the warmth from your hands to smooth the ice to make it a finished magnifying glass.

A simpler way of making a magnifying glass with ice is to take a water balloon about the size of a softball and stick it in the freezer for about an hour. Don't let it freeze solid! Take the balloon off and smack the ball of ice to let the remaining water out. You now have a perfect convex lens for starting fires.

14. Crystal Christmas ornament

Crystal Christmas ornaments have been known to focus the sun's rays and burn a hole on the couch. Weather they are manmade or natural, crystals change the shape of light that is passing through them sometimes they spread the light out, showing the different colors and sometimes the crystals focus the light like a magnifying glass. These crystals have been shaped by human hands into an art form. They are not rough like quartz that is found in the wilds. They have smooth edges and sharp corners. Try taking one of these and using it as a magnifying glass. You may have to twist it so that the sunlight is going in at an angle and being reflected into a different direction. You will know what I mean once you try it. At the very least you will have one more method of starting fires without matches.

15. Quartz

The Vikings used crystals that they found naturally in rocks to start fires. These were often a piece of quartz that they may have polished up and found worked well at magnifying sunlight. Quartz is the most common mineral on Earth. I have found many pieces of quartz in streams, embankments and as crystals inside of geodes. The only problem in using these to magnify the sun to start a fire is finding one that is a decent size and is clear enough. Keep your eye out for that sparkle in the stream or on the embankment in the bright sunlight after a good rain. Sometimes they sparkle all over and you feel like you have found a diamond mine.

16. soda can

It is a shame to say it but you can find empty soda cans almost anywhere. Even walking through a forest you may find some near a stream or in a gully. You can shine up the bottom of a soda can using steel wool, sand from the nearby stream or even a chocolate bar so that it is bright enough to reflect the sun light well enough to start a fire. Spend quite a bit of time polishing this surface to make it as shiny as possible. 20 minutes should be long enough. Don't waste your time trying to start a fire with this method unless the surface is very, very shiny.

I have started fires using soda cans a few times but you wouldn't want to bet your life on being able to start a fire this way. Align the soda can so that its shadow is smallest, that way you will know that it is pointing directly towards the sun. Make your tinder as long and narrow as possible so that you are blocking as few of the sun's rays as possible. Put the tip of your tinder at the point where the reflected sun light hits the tinder as a tight dot. Hold the tinder in this spot until it has been smoldering for 30 seconds or so. This will help ensure that it is going good enough to be blown into flames.

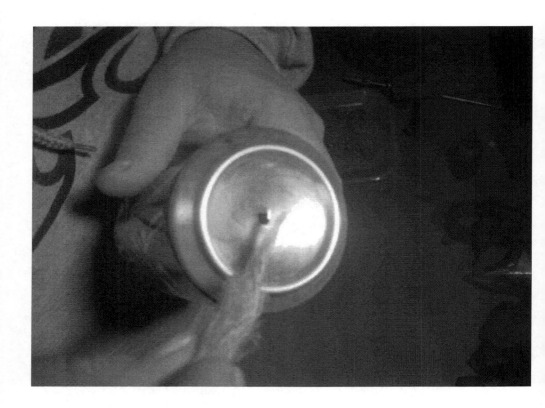

17.a round glass Christmas ornament

You can start a fire with a Christmas ornament. The round glass ones can be easily made into a perfect reflecting surface to start fires with by using needle nose pliers. Take the little cap off of the ornament, it is only held on by a small spring so gently pull on it and it will pop right out of the ornament. Take your needle nose pliers and carefully break of little pieces of the glass, working around and around until you have ½ of the ornament left. Wad up your tinder into a tight spiral that is long and stiff and you are ready to go. Lay the broken ornament on the ground and prop it up with a stone or dirt so that it is pointing directly towards the sun. Hold the tip of the tinder in the center and let the reflected sunlight work its magic. I don't know what they coat the inside of these glass ornaments with but this is a very reflective surface and works great for starting fires. Be very careful both in not cutting yourself because the edges of the glass are extremely sharp but also to not break this very fragile piece of glass. HO-HO-HO

18. Balloon

A balloon weighs almost nothing and can have many uses when camping as long as you have taken the precaution to make sure that it will not get punctured in storage. One of the many uses is to start a fire with it. You do not want to fill the balloon near bursting point but you would like it to be a good size. You want it to be manageable. You also want the balloon to be stretched until it is as thin and clear as you can make it without it bursting. I fill an average balloon until it is about 4" in diameter and then stretch it by squeezing it. Focus the sunlight through the balloon into a point of sunlight onto your tinder. You will certainly get a distorted point of sunlight but I have been able to start fires this way.

19. Brandy glass

Starting a fire using a brandy glass 1/2 full of water on a bright, sunny afternoon is actually quite easy. I say brandy glass but what I am talking about is a clear, rounded glass. The rounded shape turns the water that is inside into the perfect convex lens. The sunlight passes through the water and the outer edge of the glass to magnify the sunlight into a nice, fine pinpoint that starts tinder afire easily. You may have to tip the glass somewhat in order to get the water into the curved part of the glass. Give it a try someday when you are sitting out on the veranda.

20. Condom

To use a condom to start a fire you must first have one with you. When choosing which condoms to buy you may want to consider which ones would be good to start fires with. Although that is probably not going through your mind when purchasing condoms you would need clear, non-lubricated condoms to start a fire. You fill the condom with water and stretch it into a tight water balloon shape. Hold the open end or tie it off. Concentrate the sun's rays through your water filled condom into a pinpoint onto your tinder to get your fire started. It probably will give you a distorted point of light but it does the trick.

Condoms are not a bad thing to carry with you when hiking or camping. Not only can you start fires with them but you can also carry water and perhaps they might be needed if the right circumstances come up while out in the wilds. Better to have them and not need them than to need them and not have any.

21.Clear plastic saran wrap or sandwich bag

Clear, plastic saran wrap or a sandwich bag can be used to magnify the sun's rays to start a fire. Fill either of these with water, or even urine, and hold the pouch of liquid closed and tight. The sun's rays will be magnified but they will be distorted. Keep the pinpoint of the sun's rays onto the tinder even after it starts to smolder. Blow very gently on your smoldering tinder to try to spread the heat of the smoldering parts throughout the rest of your pile of tinder. When there is more than just a wisp of smoke and you don't think it will go out, then move the bag of liquid aside and concentrate on getting that tinder aflame. Raise it above your head and blow gently.

P.S. if you are in a survival situation and have to use this method to start fires you may want to add a few prayers in there.

22.Glasses

Eyeglasses can be used to start fires, the more powerful the correction of the lenses the better. Use a few lenses in a series, one slightly above the other in order to amplify the magnifying power. Put the tinder where the wind cannot get to it and concentrate the pinpoint of the sun's rays right into the middle of it. Adjust the lenses through experimentation. Put them closer and farther away from the tinder and try making the distance between the lenses greater or smaller. Keep the fire going once it is lit because the chances that this will work two times in a row when needed are not very good.

23. Watch crystal

You can make a magnifying lens by putting water between two watch crystals or a watch crystal and the glass on your compass. These don't work well by themselves because they are so small. By sandwiching water between two lenses, you are making them thicker and more powerful. You would use this homemade magnifying glass to concentrate the sun's rays onto tinder. Hopefully you are never in a survival situation where you will have to try this because chances are that it won't work. If your tinder is very dry and the sun is very hot and the vultures will leave you alone for a while you may end up with a fire that will keep the wolves away tonight. AHWWOOOOOO!

24. Fresnel lens

A Fresnel lens is a flat piece of plastic that has grooves engraved into it which makes the lens act like a magnifying glass. These are inexpensive, light, flat, flexible and almost indestructible. They are a great addition to your camping equipment.

Use these lenses the same as you would a regular magnifying lens. Focus the sun's rays onto a piece of tinder. Make the sun's rays as small and concentrated as possible onto the tinder by moving the tinder and lens closer and farther away from each other until you have the ideal pinpoint of sun. Don't stop when the tinder starts to smolder. Make sure that it is going very well before moving the concentrated sunlight away.

25.Binoculars or monoculars

Point your binoculars or monocular towards the sun with the large lens pointing towards the sun. DO NOT LOOK AT THE SUN THROUGH THESE! The light from the sun will be magnified onto a point about ½" from the small lens. You should not have to take these apart in order to use their magnifying glasses that are inside to focus the sun's rays. These things were designed to magnify a large viewing area into a small viewing spot. Make sure that your tinder is nice and dry and that you are gentle when blowing the smoldering tinder into flames.

26.Camera

Cameras that actually use film can be used by opening up the back where the film goes and holding the button to hold the shutter open. Remove the film and then concentrate the sun's rays from the front of the camera through the back onto your tinder.

This can only be done with cameras that use film (does anyone use those anymore?). Although this method does work you would need ideal conditions and a lot of luck to start a fire this way. This is not something to count on so carry matches with you!

By the way, film makes good kindling. It burns very well when lit with a match.

27.Telescope

You may think that mentioning a telescope is the same as binoculars or monoculars. The difference is that binoculars and monoculars do not have to be taken apart in order to use them to start fires. You should only need one of the lenses out of the telescope to start your fire. You will use this lens just the same as any other magnifying lens but how do you get it out of the telescope without damaging anything? Start at the large end of the telescope and see if anything unscrews. The one that I have has a large housing that just pulls off. Under this is a lens holding ring that unscrews. When these are off, the lens is free to fall to the ground so be careful and tip the telescope downwards and let the lens fall into your hand. Be careful to note which side of the lens was facing outward so that you can put it all together after you have started your fire. You will find that this magnifying lens is great for starting fires. It probably is of a good quality and size to capture the sun's rays into that pinpoint of heat. Clean the inside and outside of the lens before putting your telescope together. You will find that this lens is so good that the next time you go out into the wilds carrying your telescope; you might consider leaving those bulky matches at home. Well, maybe not.

28. Shooting a with a gun

First of all, don't be stupid. There are so many more, safe ways to start a fire without using guns. Try something different unless you have no other choice.

There are a few ways to start fires with guns. One way that is written about in many books is done by taking the ammunition apart. You have to pry the bullet from the cartridge, or, if you have a shotgun shell, remove the wadding and projectiles. Pour 2/3 of the powder onto your tinder and then stuff a piece of frayed clothe into the cartridge with the remaining powder. You are making a fluffy bullet. Some people believe that you can put the wad of clothe in your muzzle instead but I would be afraid of a backfire if it is in there too tightly.

Shoot the gun straight up into the air and watch for the cloth to come down. You could shoot the clothe at something large and stable, like a tree or bolder but make sure that you are quite some distance away. Don't shoot directly at your pile of tinder because all you will end up doing is scattering it in all directions. Make sure to keep an eye on this cloth and get to it quickly. You don't want to lose it and start the forest on fire. The piece of cloth will either be smoldering or on fire. Carefully place it with your tinder under your fire lay. Listen to the voice of experience when I say that this is not foolproof.

Don't be tempted to pour the extra powder on the flames if you had forgotten to do it ahead of time. You could burn yourself with a flare-up of the fire. Remember that you just want enough powder to blow the cloth a short distance. Cotton clothe would work very well for this. A wad of dry bark will do also.

Save the wadding to use as tinder. Save the shot that you take out of the bullet or shell. You can use it for a sinker for fishing or a projectile in a homemade slingshot.

If you don't have a lot of ammunition, don't try this fire starting method. Try one of the other methods first. There is a good chance that you won't be successful starting a fire with your firearm and the bullets should be saved for hunting your dinner or for signaling purposes.

You will find that a 22 shell would not have enough powder or enough blast to start a piece of wadding aflame. You might be able to do it but almost certainly would not.

The progressively burning powders in today's cartridges, especially lacking the resistance of the bullet or shot to build pressure to help the powder ignite, may make the wad come out of the muzzle partially unburned. Today's powders are slow burning regardless of caliber and this makes starting a fire today rather than 50 years ago tougher.

29. Flares

Flares are really a chemical reaction and act very much like a match but I thought they deserved their own spot in this book because they are uniquely handy in this day in age. They are easy, safe and they store well.

Flares have their obvious uses like warning people of an accident up ahead or signaling for rescue from a boat. They also are a great way to guarantee that the fire you are trying to light WILL light. This is particularly useful if you have a 1000 boy scouts watching you light the council fire or you are a firefighter trying to light a control fire.

You can make your fire lay with wood that is bigger and with more of it than you normally would use to start fires. This is because the flare will have a large, hot flame right from the beginning. Make sure to leave a good size opening at the bottom of the firelay to stick your flare into. It doesn't seem to matter how wet the wood that you are using when you start your fire with a flare.

Light the flare according to the instructions on the flare or the case that it was stored in. Try lighting one of your flares ahead of time if you have enough of them and want to be sure that everything is going to go smoothly when it is necessary to light your fire. This probably isn't necessary because it is really quite easy to light. Most flares require taking the top of the flare off and rubbing it against a part of the flare. Others require a twisting motion and still others require a flare gun.

If all you have is a flare gun to light your survival fire with then you should shoot the flare towards a pile of dirt or rocks from a long distance away. When the flare is sitting on the ground burning brightly and very hot you will have to move it to your fire lay. That is the tough part. Think this out before shooting your flare and be prepared to move it with a shovel or something else that can keep you some distance away from the flames. If all you have flare wise, is a flare gun, you may want to try a different fire making method instead.

30.Lighters

Duhhh! Lighters have got to be the first thing that comes to peoples mind when asked how to start fires without matches. Lighters come in all shapes and sizes. They can use lighter fluid or butane as fuel. They can be plastic, metal, windproof and water resistant.

I would recommend that people always have a lighter handy. Have one in your car, backpack, hunting coat and kitchen drawer. There are cheap ones that work just fine to light a fire or candle in an emergency. A lighter also makes a quick source of light if you know where one is when the lights go out. The light from the lighter can work to help you find your emergency flashlight. Keep your lighter in an inner pocket in cold weather as the cold makes the butane not work as well.

Buy lighters that have the visible view of how much fuel is left in them. This takes the guesswork out of it. If you keep a butane lighter in your coat pocket or purse, don't be surprised if all of the fuel has leaked out because the lever that lets the fuel out had something pressed up against it. An empty lighter won't light a candle. Remember though, that it will still make sparks! Put a piece of duct tape around the top of the lighter to hold the button in the up position. Duct tape is very flammable by the way.

There are good and bad ways of lighting a lighter. It is a bad idea to light it with your pointer finger or your thumb straight with the lighter. For butane type lighters, turn the lighter perpendicular to your thumb and push down on the spark wheel and keep going with the motion until your thumb rests on top of the lever that lets the butane out. Holding down on this lever will allow the fuel to keep coming out and the flame keeps going. A word of caution here, if you keep the lighter lit for too long, the metal surrounding the flame will get very hot and burn you. To light something like a campfire, camp stove or a barbeque grill with a lighter you should use the lighter to light something else on fire and then use this to light everything else. A long strip of paper that has been wound up or a foot long hand full of weeds would do well for this.

31. Yesterdays fire

Starting fires without matches isn't always easy so maybe you want to keep the fire you already have. It takes less work to keep your fire going sometimes than it takes to build another one.

"Curfew" is the English version of the French word meaning "to cover". I was brought up knowing that my curfew was THE time to be home by "or else" but it was originally the name of the metal cover or the dirt used to cover the coals of your fire to keep them going until daybreak.

The trick is to keep the wind away from the coals. They still need some air but any air that is blowing on them will shorten their life. Coals that have been buried in ashes will remain lit for many hours. The best way to try to have embers in the morning is to get a couple of good size logs burning well and then "bank them" for the evening. Spread them 6" apart and then bury them in a couple of inches of ashes. Put dirt or sand up against them on the outside but not between the logs. Have the dirt go up the sides but not on top of them. In the morning you should have good live coals to blow into flames.

Putting coals into dry, spongy wood will let them smolder for a long time. Surround the coal with ash, sand, dirt or gravel. Whatever you choose has to be clean and very dry, it wouldn't take much to put out a coal.

It is much easier to keep a fire going than to rekindle one, especially when it is wet out. In other words, do you really want to chance that your coals will go out if it is cold and rainy? If there is plenty of fuel, just keep putting wood on the fire all night long.

32. With a lit cigarette, cigar or pipe tobacco

You may think that this is a stupid or too obvious method of starting fires without matches but this is an important thing to remember if you are hiking, lost or otherwise traveling without any matches. Once you have your initial fire made using one of the other methods you may not want to go through that hassle again. Take my advice, this is worth remembering. You can carry your fire from one campsite to another simply by lighting a cigarette and using that cigarette to light another cigarette as you travel. A cigar or tobacco in a pipe would be even better because it takes longer to smoke and therefore you will be going through less of them as you travel. Once you get to your next campsite, use it to get a fluffed up pile of tinder aflame. What an easy way to carry your fire with you as you travel across the wilderness. If you are lacking matches you may find that starting your fire with your lit cigarette, cigar or pipe tobacco easier than using a bow drill or any other method of starting fires without matches.

33. Bow drill

Let's talk about the bow drill; there is a hand socket, also called a bearing block, a drill sometimes called a spindle, a fire board, and a bow which has a cord on it.

The idea of the fire drill is to create the friction necessary to create the spark of life for a fire. A vertical stick (the drill) is twirled in a notch in the fireboard creating a fine powder. Heat from the friction of wood against wood causes the powder to smolder. This smoldering powder can then be blown into flame.

You want to use wood that is not so soft that it crumbles but not so hard that it just polishes itself. You want to create dust. Woods that are good for the drill and the fire board are red cedar, white cedar, willow, yucca, poplar, basswood, tamarack, balsam fir, cypress, poplar, cottonwood, sycamore, soft maple, white pine, elm and linden. Oak is not a good type of wood to use. If you can stick your thumbnail into the wood it is probably OK to use unless it is a resinous type of wood. Resinous wood tends to polish itself.

There is a wide contradiction of what materials to use amongst experts. I have heard everything from using the same wood for spindle and fireboard, hard wood for the spindle and soft, non-resinous wood for the fireboard or a soft spindle and hard fireboard. Personally, I use the same type of wood for spindle and fireboard. You should not use black walnut, oak or chestnut or any other wood that has a gummy, resinous quality because these will not become powder easily.

You don't want your drill to be less than ¼" and not more than 1" in diameter and not less than 6" and not more than 12" long. If you have it longer or shorter, you may have problems spinning it or have it wobble a lot. You must make it easy to control. The top end of the drill should be tapered but not quite to a point make it very smooth. You don't want there to be friction on the top of your drill. You want it to spin smoothly in your socket without building up any heat. The bottom of your drill should not be smooth. A blunt end is best but you don't want it to slip out of the hole that you are drilling in the wood. You can make the edges around the blunt end slightly rounded to make it stay in the hole better. The object is friction. It is a good idea to notch the center of your spindle so that your bow string doesn't slip. You don't want the area that the bow string to go around to be smooth and round. Make sides to this area by whittling flat areas on each side. Six or eight sides like a pencil are good.

If your drill is too wide you will find it hard to get it spinning fast enough for a spark to occur. If it is too narrow of a stick then you may drill right through your fire board. You could whittle your spindle into a slight hourglass shape. It is wider at the top and bottom than in the middle. This would help the cord form sliding up or down the spindle when in use.

The fire board or hearth should be ½" to ¾" thick and a minimum of 2" by 6". You want it big enough to hold with your foot and still have room for your drill to spin. It is nice to have both the top and bottom be flat but it is not required. It will make things easier but it isn't necessary. Take your drill and hold it upright so that the side of your drill that is closest to the edge is about ½" in from the edge. This will allow the entire base of the drill to be touching the fire board and thus creating as much friction as possible. Take a mental picture or trace the bottom of the drill or spin the drill for a few seconds so that you know the exact spot it will be on your fire board. Take your knife and begin a hole for the drill. Just get it started, not very deep. If you spin the drill for a few seconds, you may be beginning the hole enough to start the hole that way. Once you have the hole started, you have to cut a groove into the side of the fire board into the center of the hole. I think your groove should look like a pie slice and be wider underneath the fire board than on top of it. There is a "rule of thirds" used to make your notch in your fireboard. The width of the notch should be about 1/3 of the diameter of the hole and should intrude 1/3 of the diameter of the hole. The hole is sometimes called the pit. This groove is where your hot dust will collect and your glowing ember will begin.

If your notch is too big then you will be losing some of the area that would create friction where your drill touches your fireboard. If the notch is too small then your dust will be forced out and be cooled off by the air around it. The notch should be cleanly cut so you can get the ember and hot dust out easily.

The socket, crown, or thimble is what you hold in your hand that holds the top of the drill. You can use a piece of wood with a hole in it but you will probably see smoke coming from this spot as you spin the drill because of all of the friction at this spot. You can put a small stone or a thimble into this hole to allow the top of the drill to spin against something that is smoother. A hard knot of a tree with a depression in it would be better because the knot doesn't wear away that easy. It becomes smooth and hard at the spot that the top of the drill is hitting. A rock that fits into your hand well, and has a natural or manmade depression in it for the top of the drill to fit into works well also. Eskimos would use a piece of serpentine or soapstone. The glass top of a coffee percolator works well as a socket. My favorite socket though is just a plain old shot glass. It fits into your hand perfectly, is ultra smooth on the inside and is so deep that you know the drill will not slip out. It is very important that whatever you use for the socket fits into your hand well or your hand fits around it well. You can put pine pitch, wild cherry sap, malleable kaolin (clay), rendered fat, nose buggers, ear wax, toe jam, wax, soap or oil on the inside of the socket to make the drill spin with less friction. Remember, this is the spot where you don't want any friction at all. The use of water as a lubricant does not work. It makes the wood swell up and bind together. Make sure that the socket fits comfortably in the palm of your hand. Not too big and not too small.

The Chippewa Indians believe that if you want the One Above to send fire, you must rub the top of your drill against either side of your nose before you try to make your fire. I don't know about you, but I am not about to argue with an Indian about starting fires.

The bow is easy to find. In fact, if you like to start fires with a bow drill while camping, take your favorite socket, fire board, drill, and cord with you out into the woods and just make another bow out of anything that you find. The drill is the longest and most easily replaced piece of the equipment.

The bow should be from 2' to 3' long and be sturdy enough not to break easily. Some people like the bow to bend so that there is a natural tension on the cord when it is wrapped around the drill. Some bows that have the ability to bend will flex slightly when you are pushing and pulling them and therefore they allow the cord to slip occasionally on the drill. You could use a bow that is slightly bent but doesn't flex when pushed or pulled. Some people prefer a stick that is straight and will be very close to the drill as it is moved back and forth. It allows a straight moving motion instead of one that arch's out a little each time. If you are having problems with your drill wobbling while you spin it with the bow, try different bow designs to find

what works best for
you.

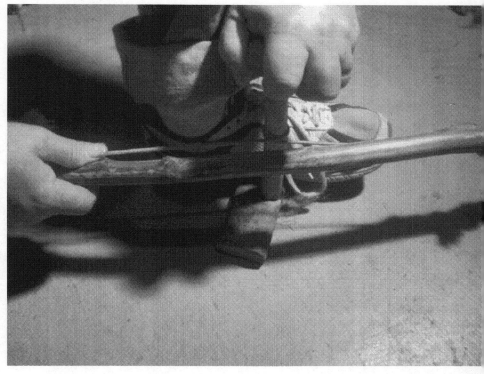

Tie your cord to each end of the bow very tightly.
You want to be able to wrap around the drill once but
to be very tight so it won't slip. You can drill a hole
through the bow to do this or just wrap the cord
around and around a few times before tying your
knot. Some people tie one end very tightly but make
the other end adjustable to re-tighten the cord when
necessary. There is a good chance that your cord will

stretch during your efforts. If the cord is too loose or too tight, your drill won't be able to spin.

The cord could be a shoelace, the string that goes around your face in a hooded sweatshirt, paracord, ¼" rope, electric cord or nylon string. Hand twisted rawhide and braintan work well for your bow cord. ½" wide buckskin works very well as a cord. Pliable leather like oiled rawhide can work well as a bow string. A piece of cordage that you made from bark, dogbane or milkweed or even a strong flexible root is good to use. Try a lightly rosined/waxed/oiled bow string. Rawhide has a good of grip and doesn't break easily. A single strand of rawhide tends to stretch so be prepared to tighten it on the end of your drill. If you are using a twisted length of rawhide you can tighten it by just making a few more twists in it.

I prefer a non-flexing bow with a cord so tight that it is actually very hard to wrap it around the drill. To wrap this around the drill you actually have to put the drill parallel to the cord and twist the drill around the cord. You want the spindle body to end up on the outside of the string. Be careful not to let go of the drill at this point or it will flip, come away from the cord and maybe hit you in the face.

To use the bow drill you can place something like a leaf or a piece of bark under the notch in the fire board to catch the hot dust and the glowing ember. This is called your welcome mat. The hot dust would get transferred over to your "birds nest". I prefer to put some tinder directly under the notch instead of a leaf or bark. Whatever you do decide to use to catch the spark, make sure that it is dry and clean and preferably, warm. This "catcher" can suck the heat out of your hot dust so that it never gets an ember. If you do use tinder to catch the hot dust, make a shallow depression in the ground for your tinder so that it doesn't get smooshed when the fireboard is placed on it. Putting the tinder under your fireboard could allow it to be wrapped up in the spindle or the tinder may get damp or smooshed. Tinder is best when it is fluffy. This is called a "coal extender". The transfer of the dust and coal can give the coal time enough to go out.

Put your left foot on top of the fire board. Using a bare foot works well with the hearth under the arch of the foot and one finger width from the edge of the hole. After you have the drill on the bow string, put the drill in the hole that was started in the fire board and place the socket on top of the drill. Keep the drill perpendicular to the fireboard. Remember that the pointy end of the drill is upwards and the blunt end is against the fire board. Hold the socket with your left hand and hold your left wrist tightly to your left shin with your left elbow hugging your left leg. Keep your left forearm as straight up and down against your shin as possible, bending your wrist that is holding the socket outwards. Keep your torso centered over the spindle and hearth hole. Stay off of your rear. You are supposed to be transferring your body weight to help with the downwards pressure.

Make sure that the drill doesn't wobble as you move the bow back and forth causing the drill to spin. Start out slowly at first, keeping the bow horizontal. Go the full length of the bow string when you pull back and forth. Concentrate on a smooth, fluid motion with your bow. "Technique" will help a lot in starting a fire with a bow drill. When the hole that the drill sits in starts to smoke, push down harder and move the bow faster. There are two things you want to take notice of by watching the smoke. Where is the smoke coming from? Is it coming from all of the way around the spindle or from the dust pile? Also, what color is the smoke? The initial smoke is white and wispy turning darker as you approach the proper temperature. The smoke you are hoping for, the smoke that an ember gives off will be a dirty, yellowish, thick smoke.

The friction between the drill and the fire board is intense now and you are creating hot wood dust. Push down very hard and spin very fast, never letting up the pressure or the rhythm. Increase the speed and downward pressure in a 2:1 ratio. The speed should increase twice as dramatically as the pressure downwards does. Do this as long as you have energy to do it. BREATHE! When you can do this no more, stop and carefully remove the drill from on top of the fire board. Do not jostle the fire board when you move your foot. Whatever coal you may have in there is fragile and can go out easily. Pick up your tinder pile and the fire board together and wave your hand over the smoldering coal. If you blow on it, it may go out. Feed it oxygen for a few seconds. Now, take your knife and scrape the coal and dust out from the notch in the fire board and set the board aside. Gently wrap your tinder pile around your coal and gently blow on your coal a couple of times and then turn it around and blow from the other side. You want your tinder pile to be getting warm and you want the heat from the coal to spread to the rest of the dust. Hold the tindle upwards. Continue to gently blow on the coal until you get a tremendous amount of smoke. The coal is extending into the tindle. Don't get your face too close because, at some point, your tinder will burst into flames.

Hopefully you have prepared your fire lay properly and are able to take the blazing tinder that is in your hand and place it under the tinder in your fire lay. Voila! You have started a fire with a bow drill.

Suggestions to make your bow drill fire making more productive;

1. Every method of friction fire starting is improved when the person dwells on style and skill instead of merely raw strength.

2. Make sure that you don't let the drill wobble. Hold your left wrist tightly against your shin and use your arm strength against your leg to hold the drill from wobbling.

3. If your drill keeps slipping out; make the hole in your fire board a little deeper. You don't want it too deep because you want wood there to create dust from.

4. If you have used this fire set before, whittle the bottom of your drill until it is flat with slightly rounded edges. If you have used it before there is a good

chance that it became rounded and smooth. You want friction and having just the edges of the bottom of your drill touching will create a lot of friction because there is all of the pressure concentrated onto the outer rim of the bottom of the drill.

5. If you get a lot of dark brown or black dust and a lot of smoke but no glowing ember then that area is getting hot but not hot enough. Try spinning your drill a little and setting it aside to dry out for a minute or so. Push down harder to cause more intense friction making the wood dust hotter. Try to run your bow drill until you just can't do it anymore, with smoke absolutely everywhere.

6. Some people put a few grains of sand between the bottom of their drill and the fire board for added friction.

7. BREATHE!

8. Clean out the angled, pie shaped groove with your knife. Make it smooth so that it is easier to get the coals away from it when the time is right.

9. Usually the embers will not combust until the dust pile rises up to the bottom of the drilled hole.

10. If you are producing light brown dust then you need to push down harder or spin the drill faster

11. If your dust is very black then you are pushing down too hard and the dust is burning

12. If the spindle keeps popping out of the bearing block then you need to make the hole in the bearing block deeper.

13. If the thong slips on the spindle then one of three things is wrong; your thong is too loose, you are pushing down on the spindle too hard or your spindle is too smooth. Try whittling it so that it has 6 or 8 sides.

14. If the thong keeps running up and down the drill stick then you are not keeping the bow perpendicular to the drill. Start your thong in the middle of the drill stick and keep your bow perpendicular and this traveling should stop.

15. If your bearing block smokes then it is made out of wood that is too soft or you are pushing down way too hard. Lubricate the bearing block

34.Hand drill

The hand drill, also called the twirling stick, is basically the bow drill without the bow and usually without the socket. This was used by Indians in California and the natives of Australia, Caroline Islands, china, Africa, and India.

I have heard of people getting a glowing coal with a hand drill in as quickly as 4 seconds. If you are not getting significant smoke after 15 seconds then you should try different wood. This is assuming that you are using the proper technique. If you spend too long trying to create a coal you may end up with blisters on your hands which will prevent you from doing other things. You do not want to hurt yourself in the wilds. Make sure that you are using very dry wood that is not too hard and that you are paying attention to technique.

Use the stem of a piece of hollow softwood for the spindle. It should have a pithy core. You can put a pinch of sand into the depression in the fireboard to increase friction.

The spindle of a hand drill should be between 15" and 30" long and about ½" in diameter, a little bit wider at the bottom than the top. If the drill is too short then you will find yourself having to reposition your hands at the top more often than you should which makes it harder to keep the pressure on the bottom tip as constant. Try making your spindle long but not so long that the top of it wobbles when your hands are near the bottom. A good size for the fireboard is 1" wide by ½" thick by 8" long and be flat on the bottom and the top.

Mullein, cattail, horseweed, and yucca make good spindles for hand drilling. Poplar, cedar, cottonwood, sycamore, willow, yucca, basswood, and box elder make good hearths (fireboard).

Prepare your fireboard the same way as you do with a bow drill. Prepare your spindle by making the bottom of it blunt with slightly rounded sides. You do not have to do anything with the top. Make sure there are no little nubs or anything else on the spindle that will injure your hands. You can leave the bark on if it is not too rough. It will give your hands more "traction" and make it so you do not have to push so hard together with your hands.

Place the fireboard on the ground with a leaf or piece of bark under where the dust will collect. Put your left foot on the end of the board keeping it as far away from the hole that the spindle is in but still holding the hearthboard very steady. Place your hands on either side of the spindle and push one hand forward while the other hand goes backwards. While push your hands together on the spindle, continue this motion while pushing down on the spindle. Try to push down relatively hard but you don't want your hands to travel to the bottom of the spindle too quickly. When your hands are about 6" above the fireboard, move one hand at a time to the top of the spindle while the other hand keeps the constant downward pressure between the drill and the fireboard. Don't let the tip of your spindle loose contact with the fireboard. Air will rush in and cool off all of your efforts. Slightly moist hands work best and you should let the weight of your torso help in applying pressure. Your hands should be arched out and very stiff.

On the other side of the coin is the advanced technique of floating while spinning your hand drill spindle. This is a method of spinning the spindle without your hands actually lowering their way down the spindle. This only gives moderate pressure downwards and is actually done only until it is time to push down with great pressure on the spindle. It is warming up the bottom of the spindle until it begins to smoke and then you really go at it with the downward pressure.

You 'float" by doing a figure eight with your hands while moving them back and forth. Your right hand is going at a downward angle towards you (fingers pointing upwards) while your left hand is going at a downwards angle away from you (fingers pointing downwards). Then you change positions and have your right hand pushing downwards and away from you (fingers pointing down) and your left hand going downwards and towards you (fingers pointing up).

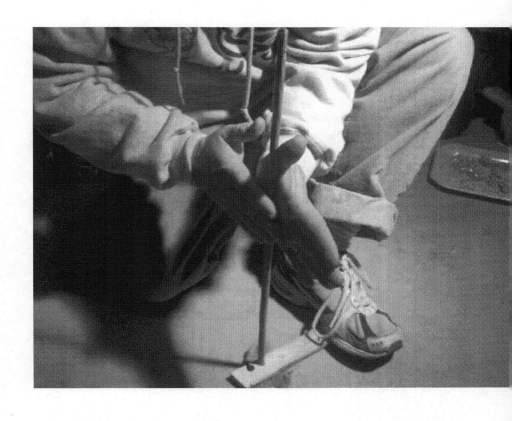

35. Fire saw

People use what is available to them for the task at hand. The fire saw works very well with bamboo which is common in many parts of the world. If you are into the whole fire experience, get some very dry bamboo and give this a try.

Take a 2' long piece of 2" bamboo and split it in half lengthwise. This is called your post or saw. Sharpen one edge of the post for the entire length.

Make the hand cross piece by taking an 8" piece of bamboo that has been split lengthwise and start cutting a groove in the outer edge, perpendicular to the length. Don't cut this slot all of the way through though. Above this groove and on the inside of the bamboo, loosen the inner part of the bamboo bark and fluff it up. Place fluffed up tinder in that location if there is no inner bark.

Kneel on both knees and place the post against your belly and the other end on the ground at about a 60 degree angle to your body. Push the bottom of the post into the ground. You don't want any wobble. Slowly start sawing the hand cross piece up and down the length of the sharpened side of the post. You want to be making the groove in your hand cross piece deeper. You should be doing this faster and faster with hard downwards motion. As always, we are trying to cause enough friction to make hot dust that starts an ember. The hot dust will accumulate on the inside of the hand cross piece where the tinder pile is sitting and waiting for the ember. Don't lift this cross piece off of the post or else your hot dust that you have created may fall out. When you see a good amount of smoke forming, rub faster and harder. You are trying to form an ember in the hot dust. I suggest that you allow the smoke to build up and keep rubbing for 30 seconds after you first see smoke.

Once you feel that you have a glowing ember in the hot dust, take a stick or knife and lift this pile of dust and ember and place the pile in your birds nest. Fold the birds nest gently around the ember and then lift above your head slightly and gently blow this into flames.

Placing the stationary piece of bamboo between two strong stakes or rocks to hold it in place will make doing all of this much more comfortable.

36. Fire string

The fire string or thong is a very unusual way of starting fires. You are making fire by producing hot dust and a coal by the friction caused by rubbing a strong string against a soft hearthboard.

You want the hearthboard to be of softer wood like cedar or basswood. Split it lengthwise but not down the entire length. You will be placing the hearthboard under your foot. The string is placed in the split opening with a wad of tinder shoved underneath it. The string is about an inch or two away from the joint of the split. Keep your foot above the joint or else the hearthboard will be pulled apart by the upwards pressure from the string. Make a notch on either side of the hearthboard for the string to slide against. The string will easily break if rubbed against sharp edges. Use the strongest, vegetable cord that you can find. Cord made from synthetic material, hide, sinew, hair all seem to melt when used. You want the string to be coarse and stronger than the hearthboard. Try cord made from dogbane, yucca, hemp, dry rattan or flax. You want it to be about ¼" in diameter and about 2' long

While kneeling on your right knee, have your left foot on top of the split part of the hearthboard. Don't allow the hearthboard to wobble at all. Make sure that your string is seated in the two notches and start sawing back and forth. You want to keep a lot of tension on the string to create the most amount of friction on the board. You will create a lot of hot dust that falls right into your tinder pile. When you see the smoke has gotten stronger and darker, stop pulling on the cord and take your tinder and blow it into flames.

The trick to making this method work is having perfectly dry materials and the right string. If your string can withstand the friction, you are sure to get the hot dust and the ember you are hoping for.

37.Pump drill

The Iroquois Indians used a pump drill to start their fires. Using momentum, inertia and mass interact causing hot dust to form a glowing ember. A flywheel is ingeniously used to make the work of spinning the shaft easier while downward pressure is applied. The idea is the same as the bow drill and hand drill but this device has a flywheel six inches or so in the air and attached to the spindle. The flywheel can be a piece of wood or stone that has a hole in the center. It is important to make sure that the flywheel is balanced so your spindle doesn't wobble.

The Indians used balsam or cedar to make their pump fire drill. Your spindle should be 18" -24" long and have a hole in the top through which a cord is passed. The cord goes down left and right and is attached to a horizontal board through which the spindle is passed. This board has a hole in it that is bigger than the spindle so that the board can move up and down the spindle easily. You don't want this board to catch on the spindle.

You place the bottom of your spindle onto the prepared fireboard the same way as you did with the bow drill. You do not need to hold a pressure block at the top of the spindle in a pump-drill set up. The fireboard is the same as the one used with the bow drill also. The hot dust and subsequent ember are made by spinning the flywheel while loosely hanging onto the horizontal hand board. The cordage will wind around the spindle until the hand board is near the top. Now, you push down gently on the hand board until it bottoms out and then you let the momentum of the flywheel continue spinning the spindle allowing the cord to wrap around the spindle, raising the handboard into the air again. Now you push down on the handboard until it bottoms out again and let the whole device rewind itself again. You always finish your downwards motion by lessoning up on the cross handle. Don't be tempted to lift the cross handle into the air. Let the momentum of the device cause the cordage to spin and thus raise the cross handle. Keep the spindle as vertical as possible but don't be tempted to hold the top of the spindle. This becomes a pumping motion where every time you push down you are creating pressure at the tip of the spindle causing friction that creates your hot dust and ember.

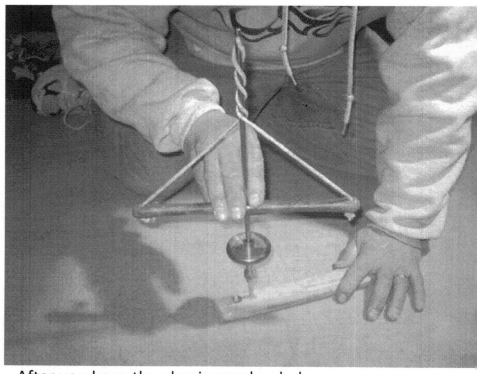

After you have the glowing ember below your fireboard, you treat it the same way as before by placing it into your birds nest and blowing it into life.

You may find with many uses that the bottom of your spindle wears away. The pump-drill took a while to make so you don't want to have to keep making them. A good solution is to make the bottom tip of the spindle replaceable. When you are initially making the spindle, create a way to connect a tip of the proper wood to the bottom. You can have a hole into which a wooden plug can be inserted or make the end flat to allow a piece of wood to be tied to it. Make sure that the connection at the bottom is strong because it will be experiencing a lot of pressure.

38. Fire plow

The fire plow, the plow stick or fire plough, is used by the natives on the Malay islands and might be the most basic form of fire starting. Can you really get more simplistic than rubbing two sticks together?

The base can be a half log that is elevated with the bottom edge emptying into a tinder pile. The plow is pushing the hot dust into the tinder pile. Stroking two pieces of wood together is far less efficient than spinning the wood together.

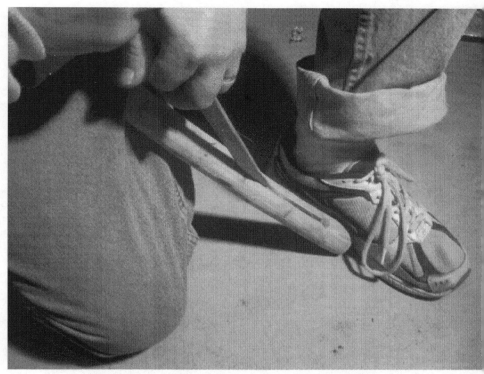

You use a harder wood as the plow and a softer wood as the hearth when using a fire plow. The plow is moved in a straight line, back and forth creating a groove in the hearth. As you move the plow forwards and backwards, you are only applying pressure in the forward motion but not lifting the plow off of the hearth in the backwards motion. You will begin to accumulate hot dust at the bottom of the stroke. You want to stop just short of the previous point so that you do not disturb the accumulated dust. You must create a growing dust pile. Eventually, you will get an ember in your dust pile as the heat from your plow pushes the hot dust to the right temperature to ignite the dust.

Try placing the end of the hearth on the ground against something that is immovable like a big rock and prop the other end up on your thigh or something else. Whatever makes you feel the most comfortable, you are about to work hard. Put the plow at about a 45 degree angle to the board. Use both hands on the plow and use brisk, sure, controlled fast strokes. Try not to disturb your dust pile that is at the end of your stroke. That is the easiest way to destroy what you have accomplished up to this point. I find that making a hole in the hearth located at the spot that my stroke ends helps me not disturb the accumulated dust.

You can make it so that your dust goes right off of the end of the board between the rock and the fireboard. You could make a notch at the end of the board for the dust to fir into and onto a leaf. You would end your stroke by hitting you plow stick against the rock.

Take the hot dust and glowing ember and put it into your birds nest as with other methods. Using a knife to do this would make your life easier...

39. Hand drill with thong

The use of a thumb-strap helps a lot with the hand drill. It is a cord that goes over or through the top of the spindle when using the hand drill. You put your thumbs through loops in the ends of the cord and can therefore apply downwards pressure easily. You can still use your hands to spin the spindle but don't have to worry about your hands going down and therefore having to be brought back up to the top of the spindle. You will be pleasantly surprised as to how much the thumb-strap helps. Were there was failure there now is success.

40. Hand drill with mouth

Place the fireboard on the ground so that it is very stable and place your foot or knee on it. Make sure that your fireboard is prepared with a notch and a hole that has been started. You do not want the spindle to slip out of this lower hole either. Anything that could go wrong could cause you serious injury. Put the spindle on the fire board and align your mouth right over the depression in the fireboard and put the spindle and mouth socket into position. Push down on the spindle and never release the pressure until you have a coal. Any slight release of pressure may cause the spindle to pop out and hurt you. As you are pushing down with your mouth, spin the spindle between your hands as quickly as you can. Adjust the amount of pressure that you are exerting on the spindle to allow you to spin the spindle. If you are pushing down too hard you will have trouble spinning the spindle. Set the spindle and mouth piece aside when you see a good amount of smoke. Carefully blow on your smoldering dust until you see the glowing coal and then carefully place this pile of dust and coal into your prepared birds nest and then blow it into flames. This method can be very dangerous. If the spindle slips out of the mouthpiece and you are pushing down with your head, you could lose an eye or poke a hole in your cheek.

I would not recommend this method because of the dangers involved. Do this at your own risk.

41. Hand drill with forehead

One person can use the hand drill and a socket. You can hold the socket in your mouth or against your forehead and exert the downward pressure with these parts of your body. To hold the spindle with your forehead you will need a stable socket that can be securely placed against your forehead. You could carve a board to fit against your head or rig up some sort of contraption using cloth and twine. Whatever you use, make sure that the socket is deep and sturdy. You do not want the top of your hand drill spindle to slip out of it.

While holding the fireboard with your foot or knee, spin the spindle with two hands by rubbing your palms back and forth on either side of the spindle. All of this time you exerting downward pressure to the spindle with your forehead. You will be collecting dust and an ember as with the regular use of the hand drill.

This may sound like a good idea but it is extremely risky. Imagine what will happen when that spindle breaks or slips out of the socket. It will poke out your eye or puncture your face. At the very least you may lose some teeth. Then starting your fire suddenly isn't that important anymore. You will have to explain to everyone how stupid you were for the rest of your life.

I would not recommend this method because of the dangers involved. Do this at your own risk.

42.2 person hand drill

Try having two people do the hand drill at the same time. As one person reaches the bottom of the spindle the next person is starting his downward pressure and spinning. This does not allow the spindle tip to cool off any and gives you a slight rest. This can be very tiring work.

Another way two people can work together with the hand drill is to have one person holding the top of the spindle with a hand socket just like you use with the bow drill. He is the person putting downward pressure on the spindle. The two people should communicate with each other so that the person exerting the pressure is giving just the right amount of pressure.

Other than these points, this method is built and used the same as the regular hand drill.

43. Egyptian bow drill

I don't know where it got its name from but the Egyptian bow drill is way easier than the normal bow drill. It doesn't allow the cord to slip at all on the drill. This allows you to put tremendous pressure downwards on the drill and create black, hot dust easily.

The difference between the Egyptian bow drill and the regular bow drill comes down to how the cord is wrapped around the drill. The drill shouldn't be short. It should be about one foot long. Your cord will have to be about a foot and a half longer than if you were going to make the standard bow drill. At the center of the cord, you tie it around the center of the drill with a clove hitch. You then wrap one side of the cord clockwise above the knot onto the drill about six times and six times counterclockwise below the clove hitch.

You use this set up the same as the regular bow drill. This method guarantees that the cord will not slip on the spindle.

44. 3 person bow drill

That pretty much describes it in a nutshell. You are dividing the work into three parts. This is a great way to teach kids how to start fires. It is easier than the standard bow drill and allows them to succeed more often. Failure always seems to stop a kid from practicing and continuing to try things and advance his skill level. They just give up and never come back to it.

You set up the 3 person bow drill the same way as the Egyptian bow drill but add about three feet to the cord. Don't use a bow to spin the spindle. Two kids will be spinning the spindle by pulling on the cord. Tie a figure 8 knot onto each end of the cord for gripping purposes. Have one kid hold the fire board, the socket and the drill in place. Have the other two kids get in a comfortable position and start a rhythm of one kid pulling their side of the cord and then the next kid pulls his side. As they get their rhythm down, they can speed up. This team work works well and is not fatiguing to any of the three kids.

45. Fire piston

The fire piston, the fire cane, or the pyropneumatic apparatus, is a manmade "machine", if you will, that compresses air so quickly and with such force that enough heat is generated to create a spark. It heats the air molecules up to 800 degrees F. This is the flash point of the tinder which makes it ignite via the heat of the compression of the air.

The first fire pistons and fire canes were probably made with bamboo with wood shavings at the bottom of the cylinder. The gasket material was probably made by wrapping a small string made of fiber or tow around the hardwood shaft. I've heard that the fire piston was invented in the South Seas and is sometimes called a South Seas Fire Maker. Once you have used the fire piston and learn to recognize its genius, try to imagine people a couple hundred years ago sitting around their campfire with the handmade tools that they had, making this awesome device. It probably was a toy or something that they discovered started fires pretty well.

The fire piston works very similar to the way a diesel engine works. Air is compressed fast enough into a small area to create a high enough temperature to ignite tinder. It's that simple and that complicated.

The fire piston has a plunger with a gasket material on it and this slides into a chamber. A good size for the chamber to be is about 3 ¼" long by 3/8" in diameter. The fit is so close that air cannot escape the chamber cavity while the plunger is pushed into it. If you push the plunger into the chamber and let go, it "boings" right back out as if there was a spring inside. The plunger has a concave cavity at its tip into which pre-charred tinder is put. I use char cloth but fungus, shredded bark or crushed charcoal also work.

Use a little lubrication on the shaft and gasket material. I use a small amount of grease but the natives probably used melted dog fat.

To use the fire piston you first put a small amount of tinder into the cavity (the natives probably used dry moss) that is at the end of the plunger. You then gently place the plunger just inside of the cavity. Hold the container in your left hand tightly and smack the plunger into it with your right hand. I've tried holding the plunger in for a second or two, keeping the pressure on it and then letting it pop out again. This works sometimes. I've also just pushed the plunger in quickly and let it pop back out. This works sometimes. I've also driven the plunger in, let it pop out, drive it in, and let it pop out a few times in a row. This works sometimes. It is very important to pull the plunger out in order to get oxygen to the ember quickly.

The friction of the air molecules creates heat and therefore the spark. Once you have a glowing ember in the tip of your plunger, gently blow on it once or twice then use a pin, needle or the tip of your knife to pluck it out and place it on more tinder in order for the glowing ember to spread. Once again, I use char cloth. Place the well established, glowing coal into a tinder pile and use your "dragon breath" to get it to burst into flames.

This is an awesome demonstration for kids. You can explain that you have just started fire with air!

Fire pistons can be found in all shapes and designs. I've seen intricately carved hardwood pistons which look cool hanging from a cord around your neck. My favorite fire piston is made of acrylic so that the kids can actually SEE the spark come to life.

46. Flashlight bulb

Do you have a "D" cell flashlight with you? You remember those don't you, before LED's were available. Take the part of the flashlight that holds the light bulb off, remove bulb and lens. Take the bulb and gently smash the glass on it without hurting the filament. Put the light bulb back into its position on the flashlight and you are ready to start a fire in a very unique way. Take a piece of cotton or oakum that you have fluffed up and place it against the filament without hurting the filament. Turn the flashlight on for two seconds and then turn it off. In that short period of time, the filament will have glowed with the heat of the resisted electrical current. This hot filament should be able to start your tinder on fire. If it did not, then try adjusting your tinder and try again. You will only have one or two tries to get your tinder lit this way before the filament burns out. This method actually works pretty well. I have been successful about 75% of the time.

47.9volt and steel wool

An easy and exciting way of starting a fire without matches is with steel wool and a battery. You take a small bit of steel wool and fluff it up a bit. You don't want it all tight together. Use the finest steel wool you can find. "0000" steel wool works very well. Wrap the fluffed up piece of steel wool with some fluffed up jute twine and you are ready to go. Touch the negative and positive terminals of a 9 volt battery to the steel wool and when you see the wool start to glow, set the battery down and gently start blowing on the glowing part of the steel wool. The glow will spread and the whole mass of wool and twine will get warmer and warmer. Steel wool actually burns very well by itself but the twine catches faster. With some gentle blowing your tinder will eventually burst into flames. Be ready for this because it is kind of sudden. Remember to have your fire lay ready so you can place this tinder that is on fire in your hands in the right spot to get your campfire going.

You don't have to hold the battery to the steel wool just touch it and then pull it away. If you hold it there you will be shorting out the battery and it won't

last very long. Just touch the battery and then pull it
away.

48. Car cigarette lighter

Your cars cigarette lighter has a built in resistor in it. When the lighter is pushed in, the electricity from your cars battery runs through the lighter and builds up resistance to the point where the lighter is glowing. When the lighter pops out, touch a fine piece of tinder to the glowing end to catch the tinder afire.

The obvious problem with starting fires this way is that you have to take the glowing, hot cigarette lighter from its holder outside to light your tinder. It is not like the lighter is heavy but it is very hot. Use this method to light some dry grass and then take the grass and light your charcoal in your grill when you had brought all of the hot dogs, macaroni salad and beans but no matches.

49. Potassium permanganate and antifreeze

Potassium Permanganate used to be carried in everyone's camping first aid kit. It is a mild antiseptic and could be used to purify water. It can also be used to start fires a few different ways. Be careful though because it makes a purple color residue that permanently stains whatever it touches.

If you take one tablespoon of potassium permanganate and put it on a piece of paper and put three drops of antifreeze or brake fluid from your car onto it, wrap it up tightly into a ball, then in a minute or so the wad will burst into flames. The chemical reaction reaches at least 450 degrees F which is the flashpoint of paper.

This is a very cool demonstration to watch but stand back a little. Sometimes the reaction is so violent that the wad of paper may pop because of the pressure and rapid expansion. I usually don't tell people what the chemicals are so that some kid doesn't store these under his bed and start his house on fire. These chemicals should be kept away from each other in storage. All they have to do is touch and you will get a fire.

50. Potassium permanganate and sugar

I have taken one part potassium permanganate and one part sugar and mixed them together thoroughly and put this mixture into a small plastic bottle that I keep with my fire demonstration equipment. Shaking this mixture does nothing but if you pour a pile onto a rock and grind the mixture into a powder by sliding another rock across it the chemicals start a fire that burn across the pile slowly. It smells like marshmallows too. It is the grinding action that starts the whole chain reaction. When it does begin to burn, it will burn slowly so don't be afraid of it bursting into flames. What you should be afraid of is getting the potassium permanganate onto your clothing. It makes a permanent purple stain.

Well, there you go fifty methods of starting a fire without matches. Hopefully you learned something new here. Remember to be careful. Fire is an amazing thing but is very dangerous and certainly not something to play with. Just because a lot of these methods are fun doesn't mean that you should take any of this lightly. Check out my fire book when it comes out and learn a lot more. I think there are 40 or 50 more methods described in there that I didn't have room for in this book.

I would also like to mention that there are Boy Scout Troops in your area that need help. Each of us knows some skill that can be taught to the boys. Please go and spend an hour teaching what you know to the boys so that future generations can benefit from your knowledge. Thanks from all of us in scouting.

Made in the USA
San Bernardino, CA
16 May 2016